Wrapped Up
Companion Journal

God's
Ten
Gifts
for
Women

TERESA TOMEO & CHERYL DICKOW

SERVANT
BOOKS

PUBLISHED BY FRANCISCAN MEDIA
Cincinnati, Ohio

Cover design by Mary Ann Smith
Cover image © Image Source | SuperStock
Book design by Mark Sullivan

ISBN 978-1-61636-488-5

Published by Servant Books,
an imprint of Franciscan Media
28 W. Liberty St.
Cincinnati, OH 45202
www.FranciscanMedia.org
www.ServantBooks.org

Printed in the United States of America.
Printed on acid-free paper.

12 13 14 15 16 5 4 3 2 1

contents

A Personal Note From Cheryl

My college-aged son suggested that I start "tweeting."

I had to laugh. I would have bet cold hard cash that this young man listened to very little of what I said while he was growing up. So for him to suggest that anyone else would listen to what I had to say really caught me by surprise.

Writing a book is sort of like that. Do I really have anything worthwhile to say? Have I been given any insights valuable enough to share? Am I entitled to take up someone's precious time with my writings?

It's a considerable responsibility—one I don't take lightly.

As I asked the Holy Spirit to guide me, one truth seemed particularly essential to what I was writing: Learning about our connection to the past allows us to build our homes on rock, just as Jesus has advised we do (see Matthew 7:24–27). In building our homes on rock, he says, we will be able to withstand whatever comes against us.

I hope the women whose lives I share with you in *Wrapped Up* will become special to you in the pages of this *Companion Journal*. I see them as being truly alive and having significantly affected my time on earth while I sojourn toward my eternal life in heaven. In connecting with them and with the rich history of *your* faith, my prayer is that you will build your home on the foundation that will not wash away: rock.

And I guess, in the end, that is exactly what I would tweet:

Build your home on the solid rock of feminine strength through unshakable faith. #wrappedup.

A Personal Note From Teresa

In Luke 5:1–11 Jesus tells Simon Peter to "put out into the deep." St. Peter's reaction is at first one of surprise. After all he and the other disciples were experienced fishermen. Jesus's instruction was not the normal way of catching fish. St. Peter told Jesus they had been "toiling all night and caught nothing." But the Gospel here also tells us that St. Peter, despite his own doubts, listened to Jesus—and, of course, they ended up catching so many fish that their nets were almost destroyed.

With this *Companion Journal* we hope you will follow the Lord's same instruction to Simon Peter and put out into the deep. Here is your chance to dive even deeper into the warm waters of God's love. Maybe you have been in a relationship with God for a while. Maybe you are doing everything you think you're supposed to be doing in order to have a better spiritual life in general, but something isn't clicking quite yet. Or maybe you're just looking for more. This journal is designed to lead you into further study and reflection about the gifts God has for you. We have designed the summaries, questions, and reflection resources with discussions in mind—discussions you may want to have within a study group, with a circle of friends, between you and the Lord, or all the above. So come on in. The water's fine. Let this journal be your net. Throw it out into the deep end and just see what Jesus has in store!

GUIDELINES | *for leaders*

1. Each participant should bring a Bible, the *Catechism*, her *Wrapped Up* book, this journal, a pen, and any other items requested by the leader to help the group run smoothly while allowing for personal revelations and insights to be shared.

2. Some tips:
   - *Prayer requests:* Keep this short and simple; a prayer request can quickly turn into a conversation.
   - *Introductory prayers:* Use the prayers at the beginning of the Companion Journal chapters or encourage participants to take turns bringing in a prayer to share.
   - *Concluding prayers:* A particularly powerful concluding prayer is the Prayer to the Holy Spirit. It is also meaningful to have the women take turns offering a blessing to the group as a way to conclude the gathering.
   - *Refreshments:* You might choose to ask different participants to provide light snacks each week, but keep it simple!

3. It is imperative for the leader to gently and lovingly guide the discussion, help keep everyone on topic, and maintain an awareness of time.

4. Prior to the start of each gathering, the leader should assign different participants to locate and bookmark one or more of the Scripture verses and *Catechism* excerpts for the upcoming chapter. The participants will then take turns reading the verses throughout the gathering; encourage discussion on as many as time allows and suggest that the participants to meditate upon them throughout the week.

5. Participants should read through the designated material on their own during the week prior to the gathering. Alternatively, the leader may choose to have the participants do their reading as a group, taking turns, during the gathering.

6. The questions at the end of each chapter of the *Companion Journal* are excellent discussion starters for each participant after reading the corresponding chapter in *Wrapped Up*. They are meant to introduce concepts for contemplation and should be a springboard for a life lived in awareness of the ten gifts.

7. Participants can use a separate journal to record their insights during the week as they meditate upon the material. The few lines provided within the *Companion Journal* for takeaways will provide the basis for more focused journal writing. Some of these entries might be shared; others might remain private.

8. This is essentially a ten-week course, but it can be divided any number of ways. One suggestion is to schedule a break between weeks three and four and then again between weeks seven and eight. Any arrangement can be made at the leader's discretion. Look ahead at a calendar to accommodate any major holidays, if necessary.

9. The leader should ask the Holy Spirit to help her guide the group's participation. There is tremendous flexibility in how the *Wrapped Up Companion Journal* can be utilized. Through prayer, discernment, confidence, and joy, each leader will create a blessed time in her own way!

GUIDELINES | *for participants*

Participating in a group study—whether large or small—is always an anointed opportunity. There are a number of things to keep in mind so that you will get the most out of your study time.

1. Follow the leader's decision in regard to how the study will be run. This means that if you are expected to read from the book in preparation for your time with the group, consider this an important task and accomplish it! Be committed to the process and the group. The same goes for possible "homework." If you are asked to answer questions, make journal entries, study Scripture verses, or read from the *Catechism,* consider these important tasks and accomplish them as requested.
2. Honor and respect all participants and their insights. Trust that the leader will get the group back on track if conversations become too fragmented or stray from the topic at hand, and do your best to stay focused as a participant—not contributing to runaway conversations while still allowing the Holy Spirit to move you and to respond as appropriate.
3. Along with the group's prayers, it is always a blessing to specifically prepare yourself for your study time. Invite the Holy Spirit to be part of your speaking and your listening. Ask for guidance and help with any personal issues you may be facing and invite the Holy Spirit to show you how the lessons are applicable to your personal journey. Seek wisdom, compassion, and understanding so that the fruits of this study will be evident and life-changing for you and your relationship with God.

4. Always thank the leader and the other participants for their time and for their willingness to be part of your journey. If you ask, the Holy Spirit will give you the right words.

5. Remember that this is a joyful time, but also a time in which you will be shown the vulnerabilities of others through what they will share. See each participant through Christ's eyes and create a place in your heart for them, knowing that your time together is certainly ordained by God.

chapter one

THE
GIFT
OF
GOD'S
LOVE

A Prayer to Begin...

Father, we thank you for the great gift of your love! As we begin to experience your love in new and deeper ways, teach us to open our hearts and share that love with the world. We know that our confidence and self-esteem come from knowing your love. Help us to be aware of those around us who may be struggling with negative feelings about themselves. Bring us opportunities to share true love and acceptance with them. Amen.

TIMELESS | TRUTHS *Cheryl*

Then God said, "Let us make man in our image, after our own likeness"...male and female he created them.... And God saw everything that he had made, and behold, it was very good.

—Genesis 1:26–27, 31

God who created man out of love also calls him to love—the fundamental and innate vocation of every human being. For man is created in the image and likeness of God who is himself love.

—CCC, 1604

Women are created to be great receivers of God's immense love. The same spiritual DNA that makes them nurturers and givers is the same spiritual DNA that makes them the ideal receptacle of God's love. However, if a woman decides she is unworthy to receive the gift of God's love, she can't really serve him well. Instead of being a receiver, she will fall into merely doing, and she will try in futile ways to fill the empty place in her soul meant to be filled with God's love. To become a passive vessel for God to fill with love is an idea whose time has come; it is the divine design that must be embraced in order for a woman to live her life, her vocation, to its fullest—*and then to be that love to others.*

Love is often mistaken for something it's not, and what love really is often goes unrecognized. When we get to the bottom of what love is, it is much easier for each and every woman to be "love." This is because love is not a Hollywood fairy tale but a commitment. While it manifests in a gentle spirit, it is also present in our sisters who seem more like bulls in a china shop than anything else.

When a woman proclaims that she loves her husband and children, this isn't to say that she is always enamored of them. Her commitment to her family carries her through when her feelings wane. God wasn't wild about his people's transgressions either, but he still promised an answer, a Savior. Why? Because God loved his people. In other words, God's commitment never waned even when the Israelites gave him good cause to withdraw that commitment.

God's love is often called "*agape*" love. It is a love that could send a most beloved Son to the world for crucifixion. It is completely selfless and cannot be earned, bought, traded, or sold. Agape love is unconditional love. God's love for us, his creations, reflects his commitment to us.

Love, then, as a daily goal, is both ours to attain and ours to embrace. Whether she has been called to the vocation of marriage, or a consecrated life, or a life as a single woman, every woman is able to be "love" to those in her life.

SCRIPTURES | *for reflection*

Look up each verse and read it slowly and prayerfully. What do you sense God saying to you about his love for you? Write your answers in your journal.

Psalm 51:6

_____

_____

Ephesians 4:1–2

_____

_____

1 John 4:7

_____

_____

CATECHISM EXCERPTS | *for reflection*

Now do the same for the *Catechism* excerpts. Note in your journal your insights and anything new you haven't realized before about God's love.

CCC, 368

_____

_____

CCC, 2011

_____

_____

CCC, 2658

_____

_____

TIMELESS | TRUTHS
Cheryl

Discussion Questions

1. What do you see as the three most important characteristics of a matriarch? Why? (These do not need to have been identified in this chapter but can be based upon your own experiences or understanding.)

2. Is there someone you admire today that you consider a modern-day matriarch? Describe what makes you choose this person.

3. Do you have one or more of these characteristics? List them and journal about how they manifest in your life. Which ones do you need to work on?

4. Describe how and when you've experienced true joy in your earthly journey toward heaven.

5. Now think of a time when you have felt joyless. What were the reasons? What did you do to change this?

6. Do you allow yourself to be loved by God? If so, what have been the results? If not, what has stopped you, and how can you change this?

7. As you show love to your family, friends, coworkers, and those in your Church and community, how do you from becoming overwhelmed or exhausted? What can Sarah's example teach you?

8. List an experience you've had where circumstances were not as you had hoped. How did God use this in your life to purify and shape you?

MY | PERSONAL | TAKEAWAY

_____

_____

_____

_____

_____

_____

_____

_____

_____

_____

_____

_____

_____

_____

_____

_____

_____

_____

_____

_____

_____

_____

_____

TIMELY | TRUTHS   *Teresa*

I praise you, for I am wondrously made.

—Psalm 139:14

Being in the image of God the human individual possesses the dignity of a person, who is not just something, but someone.

—CCC, 357

For many of us, even those of us who believe in God, being able to think of ourselves as loveable, wanted, or even somewhat special is barely a blip on our personal radar screen. Instead, because of a variety of negative influences and sources, we have come to accept a very unfavorable view of ourselves. In addition to the personal baggage we carry, the other signals constantly received or detected on the private sonar remind us that unless we can feed the family with a fabulous "yummo" Rachel Ray dinner in thirty minutes or less, raise perfectly polite and poised Harvard-bound children, look like Angelina Jolie, and earn at least a six-figure income, we might as well throw in the towel because we just aren't "all that and a bag of chips," as a good friend of mine likes to say.

Instead of tuning into the latest talk show, or spending too much time listening to the nightly news, let's remember that God has written us a lengthy love letter, the Bible. Here we can get a dose of true reality—we can learn what the one who created us says we are really worth.

SCRIPTURES | *for reflection*

Look up each verse and read it slowly and prayerfully. What do you sense God saying to you? Write your answers in your journal.

Jeremiah 1:5

_____

_____

John 1:12

_____

_____

1 John 4:16

_____

_____

CATECHISM EXCERPTS | *for reflection*

Now do the same for the *Catechism* excerpts. Note in your journal your insights and anything new you haven't realized before about God's love.

CCC, 343

_____

_____

CCC, 364

_____

_____

CCC, 1701

_____

_____

TIMELY | TRUTHS   *Teresa*
Discussion Questions

1. When was the last time you accepted a compliment without trying to dismiss it or make light of it?

2. What kind of struggles have you had regarding your body image? List any current issues as well as those you may have wrestled with in the past. What steps have you taken to overcome them?

3. How would you describe yourself physically?

4. How does knowing you were lovingly created by God affect the way you view yourself—not only on the inside, but outwardly as well?

5. If you have a daughter, how are you teaching her to view herself? In what areas do you see her struggling?

6. What is the basis for any regular negative thinking that might be occurring in your life? Past hurts? Family pressures and responsibilities? Outside sources such as media influence and peer pressure?

7. When you think of God creating you, what three things are you most grateful for?

8. List one thing you can do this week to demonstrate that you are the temple of the Holy Spirit.

MY | PERSONAL | TAKEAWAY

_____

_____

_____

_____

_____

_____

_____

_____

_____

_____

_____

_____

_____

_____

_____

_____

_____

_____

_____

_____

_____

_____

_____

chapter two

THE
GIFT
OF
FORGIVENESS

A Prayer to Begin...

Merciful God, how grateful I am for the gift of your forgiveness! You have freely welcomed me fully into your kingdom. Help me to really understand the price you paid to make this forgiveness possible. Show me how I can offer this gift to others, especially those who have hurt me. As you have forgiven me, let me forgive others! Amen.

TIMELESS | TRUTHS   *Cheryl*

Who is a God like you, pardoning iniquity and passing over transgression for the remnant of his inheritance? He does not retain his anger forever because he delights in mercy. He will again have compassion on us, he will tread our iniquities under foot. You will cast all our sins into the depths of the sea.

—Micah 6:18-19

Only the Spirit by whom we live can make "ours" the same mind that was in Christ Jesus. Then the unity of forgiveness becomes possible and we find ourselves "forgiving one another, *as* God in Christ forgave" us.[1]

—CCC, 2842

Forgiveness truly one of the gifts we give ourselves. When we allow ourselves to forgive and be forgiven, we allow ourselves to embrace a treasure that has reward beyond measure. Forgiving isn't forgetting, nor is it letting someone get away with something. Instead, forgiveness—both the giving and the receiving—is actually an act of mercy, and thus something to which we are all called because of our baptismal vows.

I had been truly hurt by someone with whom I felt I had a strong personal and professional relationship. I had given my all and had come to see her more as a friend than as a colleague. So I was crushed when she made a decision that both harmed my business and also cut me personally to the core. I struggled to get over the emotional pain, which was only made deeper by the financial impact of her decision. Her words, "This isn't personal; this is business," only made matters worse.

As time went by I prayed and begged God to fill my heart with forgiveness for this woman whom I knew to be a faith-filled sister in the Lord. Indeed, I felt that I had reached the point of forgiveness when an incident occurred that made me realize that full forgiveness in my heart had yet to be obtained. I asked my spiritual director to explain to me what forgiveness really looked like since I had clearly not gotten there though I thought I had.

She explained that forgiveness exists on many levels and that it often occurs over time. We are, after all, very human; we can't turn things on and off like a light switch. She said that God allows this to happen so that, at each occurrence of a new feeling or thought, we are able to offer it to him the same way that he offered us forgiveness, and thus release that particular piece of the situation. She helped me see that it wasn't that I hadn't forgiven when I thought I had; but that over time all the pieces of the wound would surface, and each piece would allow greater depth of the forgiveness that I was seeking to experience toward this woman. The way my spiritual director explained it was that our wounds often are so deep that God protects us in allowing us to tackle them bit by bit. In this way, we aren't overwhelmed by our attempts to be superhuman in the forgiveness department; rather, each new revelation of a pain that still exists becomes an opportunity for us to grow in holiness as we become whole.

So when you struggle with forgiveness, thinking you have attained it only to see that you haven't, it is best not to be too hard on yourself, but instead to see that God is simply allowing you to go slowly to your center and exist, more fully, in the depths of it with him.

SCRIPTURES | *for reflection*

Look up each verse and read it slowly and prayerfully. What do you sense God saying to you? Write your answers in your journal.

Numbers 14:18–19

_____

_____

Luke 11:4

_____

_____

Ephesians 4:32

_____

_____

CATECHISM EXCERPTS | *for reflection*

Now do the same for the *Catechism* excerpts. Note in your journal your insights and anything new you have discovered about forgiveness.

CCC, 977–978

_____

_____

CCC, 1829

_____

_____

CCC, 2843

_____

_____

TIMELESS | TRUTHS *Cheryl*
Discussion Questions

1. Have you asked for and accepted the forgiveness you have been given in Christ? If so, what have the results been? If not, what has stopped you?
2. Why is it important to accept the gift of Christ's forgiveness?
3. What steps can you take, right now, to accept this gift?
4. Is there someone in your life you have been unable to forgive? If so, why? How can you remedy the situation?
5. Have you freely forgiven someone who has asked you to forgive them? How did that feel? How was God part of that process?
6. Think of a time when you have offended someone. Were you able to ask their forgiveness? How did their response affect you?
7. How do you perceive God's mercy? Do you feel it is for everyone but you? Does it have limits? Do you sense a need for it?
8. Is there a person who needs your forgiveness, even though they haven't asked for it? How might you offer them this gift?

MY | PERSONAL | TAKEAWAY

TIMELY | TRUTHS   *Teresa*

While we were yet helpless, at the right time Christ died for the ungodly. Why, one will hardly die for a righteous man though perhaps for a good man one will dare even to die. But God shows his love for us in that while we were yet sinners Christ died for us.

—Romans 5:6–8

During his public life Jesus not only forgave sins, but also made plain the effect of this forgiveness: he reintegrated forgiven sinners into the community of the People of God from which sin had alienated or even excluded them.[2]

—CCC, 1443

If we identify ourselves as Christians, then, whether we like it or not, forgiveness is the *main* part of the equation. Our entire faith is built on it. We needed forgiving and saving, so God sent a savior. Our Redeemer redeemed us on the cross while we were *still* sinners, as it says in Romans 5:8. That said, in today's "Gotcha" or "I'm gonna getcha" world of online bullying, road rage, and mass shootings, forgiveness is hardly at the top of the "good citizen" priority list.

It's nice to know, though, that the gift of forgiveness is also good for our physical and psychological well-being. Over the past ten years, there has been more and more research concerning what is known as the "science of forgiveness." One study by the University of Michigan's Institute for Social Research found that people who forgive not only themselves but others experience "reduced feelings of restlessness, nervousness, and hopelessness." Other studies show forgiveness is connected to lower blood pressure and heart rates.[3]

SCRIPTURES | *for reflection*

Look up each verse and read it slowly and prayerfully. What do you sense God saying to you? Write your answers in your journal.

Ephesians 2:4–7

_____

_____

Colossians 3:12–13

_____

_____

Hebrews 8:12

_____

_____

CATECHISM EXCERPTS | *for reflection*

Now do the same for the *Catechism* excerpts. Note in your journal your insights and anything new you haven't realized before about forgiveness.

CCC, 982

_____

_____

CCC, 1441

_____

_____

CCC, 2840

_____

_____

TIMELY | TRUTHS
Teresa
Discussion Questions

1. Do you experience restlessness, nervousness, or hopelessness? If so, could these feelings be related to a lack of forgiveness in your life?

2. Has there been a time in your life where you've had to forgive yourself? What were the circumstances, and how difficult was this for you to do?

3. Do you know of someone who is having a tough time forgiving herself (or himself) for something serious they were responsible for? How might you help this person accept the gift of forgiveness?

4. If you are married, how has the ability to extend forgiveness made an impact on your relationship with your spouse?

5. What kinds of things do you find yourself having to forgive in your spouse?

6. How has a lack of forgiveness (on either your part or on someone else's) affected your relationships at home, at work, or in your community?

7. Do you go to confession regularly? If not, why not?

8. When you do go to confession, what is the result? What are some of the benefits of this sacrament for you personally?

MY | PERSONAL | TAKEAWAY

_____
_____
_____
_____
_____
_____
_____
_____
_____
_____
_____
_____
_____
_____
_____
_____
_____
_____
_____
_____
_____
_____

chapter three

THE
GIFT
OF
ALLOWING
GOD
TO
BE
GOD

A Prayer to Begin...

Dear Lord, as the God of the universe, you are certainly trustworthy and capable of knowing what's best for me and for those I love. As I surrender my stubbornness about how I think things should go, you are able to open my eyes to new directions I might have missed. Thank you for the peace that comes from allowing you to be you! Amen.

TIMELESS | TRUTHS   *Cheryl*

And Mary said, "Behold, I am the handmaid of the Lord; let it be to me according to your word."

—Luke 1:38

God is the sovereign master of his plan. But to carry it out he also makes use of his creatures' cooperation. This use is not a sign of weakness, but rather a token of almighty God's greatness and goodness. For God grants his creatures not only their existence, but also the dignity of acting on their own, of being causes and principles for each other, and thus of cooperating in the accomplishment of his plan.

—CCC, 306

Fear is the opposite of trust. Fear creates a foundation from which evil can grow and undermine all God intends for you in your life. Maybe you've been afraid that the economy won't sustain you in your retirement or that you have not chosen the correct method of parenting. It really doesn't matter how you finish the sentence, *I am afraid of...*, because the sentence itself is an indicator that you do not trust in God, his timing, or his wisdom.

The only way to combat fear is to make a conscious point of trusting God, of allowing God to be God. This isn't to say that we sit and back say, "If God wants me to have money I trust in him and am sure he will blow it in through my open windows." Trusting in God and allowing him to act in everything never translates into irresponsible behavior. Allowing God to be God means living life as God intends, obeying his commandments, honoring the life that he has so graciously given each of us in a way that clearly shows the world what it means to live as a Christian.

So what does trust look like where we allow God to be God? The best way to describe this trust, this release, is to imagine the exact opposite of fear. Imagine all the ways fear has been a motivator for your behavior or decisions you've made and then see how trusting God would have changed things. Trusting God really makes all the difference in how we act and react.

Allowing God to be God frees a woman to be what God intended her to be. She can trust him in all things, knowing he will work them for her good. She will experience times of joy and times of anguish. She will know love and loss. But through it all, her trust in God remains constant because she is allowing God to be God. She believes and she knows that he remains faithful to her and that her recompense will be in heaven.

SCRIPTURES | *for reflection*

Look up each verse and read it slowly and prayerfully. What do you sense God saying to you? Write your answers in your journal.

Genesis 1.26

_____

_____

Ephesians 1:4–7

_____

_____

Hebrews 12:28

_____

_____

CATECHISM EXCERPTS | *for reflection*

Now do the same for the *Catechism* excerpts. Note in your journal your insights and anything new you haven't realized before about allowing God to be God.

CCC, 489

_____

_____

CCC, 1730

_____

_____

CCC, 2843

_____

_____

TIMELESS | TRUTHS   *Cheryl*
Discussion Questions

1. Do you pray "so that" prayers, subtly (or not so subtly) directing God to accomplish the outcomes you decide are the right ones?

2. What would be a more effective way of praying about something you think should happen?

3. What are the advantages of allowing God to be God in your life?

4. What kind of action does this require of you?

5. Is there someone in your life who models letting God be God? How?

6. What happens if you don't allow God to be God in your life? What are the day-to-day experiences of retaining control of your life and its circumstances?

7. How does letting God be God differ from being resigned and passive?

8. How would you finish the sentence, "I am afraid that...."? How can you turn this fear into a radical trust in God?

MY | PERSONAL | TAKEAWAY

_____
_____
_____
_____
_____
_____
_____
_____
_____
_____
_____
_____
_____
_____
_____
_____
_____
_____
_____
_____
_____
_____
_____
_____

TIMELY | TRUTHS   *Teresa*

Come now, you who say, "Today or tomorrow we will go into such and such a town and spend a year there and trade and get gain" whereas you do not know about tomorrow. What is your life? For you are a mist that vanishes. Instead you ought to say, "If the Lord wills, we shall live and we shall do this or that."

—James 4:13–16

Divine providence works also through the actions of creatures. To human beings God grants the ability to cooperate freely with his plans.

—CCC, 323

You might think the verses above from James 4 are encouraging us not to make plans, or balance our checking accounts, or take care of ourselves physically. After all, if we are going to let God be God and if God is really in charge, what difference does any of that make? Upon further pondering and reflecting, though, I've realized that saying "God willing" is a verbal acknowledgment of whom we put first in our lives. We need to recognize that every breath we take is only given to us because God is allowing it. It's okay to move forward in our lives, to get up every morning and go to work or take care of our children and our homes. We do this knowing that God is guiding our every step.

"God willing. If the Lord wills, we shall live and we shall do this or that." Yes, we can dream. Yes, we can plan. First, though, we must make sure we recognize that nothing we do happens without God's allowing it. Saying those words remind us to always look upward and let God be God. And if our plans are in line with his, then *God willing,* it will be.

SCRIPTURES | *for reflection*

Look up each verse and read it slowly and prayerfully. What do you sense God saying to you? Write your answers in your journal.

1 Thessalonians 5:18

In all things give thanks

_____

_____

Proverbs 16:1–3

_____

_____

Job 1:20–22

_____

_____

CATECHISM EXCERPTS | *for reflection*

Now do the same for the *Catechism* excerpts. Note in your journal your insights and anything new you haven't realized before about allowing God to be God.

CCC, 2062

_____

_____

CCC, 2115

_____

_____

CCC, 303

_____

_____

TIMELY | TRUTHS   *Teresa*

Discussion Questions

1. Have there been events in your life, or in the lives of your ancestors, that seemed tragic or unpleasant at the time but led to a direction your life would not have taken otherwise? Describe them briefly.

2. What lessons have you learned when things didn't turn out the way you'd hoped?

3. If you have a big goal, do you sense that God has given it to you? How do you plan to reach this goal?

4. Does your faith make a difference in your approach to dreams and goals? How?

5. Do you have a particular phrase you use to remind yourself that God is God? Maybe "Lord willing" or something similar? Jot down a few possibilities.

6. What are some ways you can keep yourself and your family from being overly influenced by today's culture, which doesn't tend to recognize God's hand much anymore?

7. When you think of letting God be God in your life, do you have a sense of anticipation, or one of dread? Why?

8. Is there a situation or something you are longing for right now that you've been holding on to? Take some time to pray about this and give it to God.

MY | PERSONAL | TAKEAWAY

chapter four

THE
GIFT
OF
A
JOYFUL
ATTITUDE

A Prayer to Begin...

My heavenly Father, in your Son I am able to know true joy.
Through his life, death, and resurrection I have gained eternity.
This knowledge alone sustains and inebriates me. It puts everything
into perspective—a perspective from which I can most joyfully serve
you through serving others. I am honored to be your joyful servant!
Amen.

TIMELESS | TRUTHS   *Cheryl*

Awake, awake, Deborah!

Awake, awake, utter a song!

—Judges 5:12

Such holy women as Sarah, Rebecca, Rachel, Miriam, Deborah, Hannah, Judith, and Esther kept alive the hope of Israel's salvation.

—CCC, 64

Just like Deborah, in our own personal journey we will have some sort of war that we wage—it may be a war against illness, sadness, unemployment, addiction, or any sort of trouble—and just like Deborah, we can have the assurance that God will be with us, he will strengthen us, and he will guide us if we remember to reach into the depths of our hearts and sing his praises. Judge Deborah shows us that keeping a joyful attitude is a wonderful way to serve God. It is during those most difficult times that having a joyful attitude will lift us up and animate us—and permit us to rightfully praise God.

In her zeal to serve God, in the ways her joyful attitude gives life to all that she does, Deborah was able to be a successful businesswoman, a righteous judge, a valiant warrior, and a devoted wife. She shows us that the armor we are called to wear (see Ephesians 6:11) is meant to house the joyful attitude in which we are called to serve.

During my teaching career, one of my favorite pictures that hung on my classroom walls was a picture of a laughing Jesus. I found great joy in that picture. We don't often see Christ with a smile on his face, and this particular picture evoked a whole new set of emotions for me when I thought of Christ.

As the years went by, and as I grew in my faith, I began to realize that even if Christ did not have a smile on his face, his heart was filled with joy. The more I understood his great love for each of us, the more I knew that we all brought him joy. He didn't need to be laughing for me to know I, personally, was the cause of some of the joy he undoubtedly felt in his heart—regardless of the circumstances that his love for me brought into his life.

It didn't take long to recognize that this logic could—and should—be reversed as well. My love for him ought to be the cause of a steady stream of joy in my heart, regardless of my circumstances. This should be the foundation we step on, like a huge, high rock ledge overlooking a cavernous gully, when we need to look past whatever quagmire we may feel has us in its grips. Having a joyful attitude can be the only logical way to exist when we really see that we are wrapped in the arms of Christ.

SCRIPTURES | *for reflection*

Look up each verse and read it slowly and prayerfully. What do you sense God saying to you? Write your answers in your journal.

Psalm 30:11–12

_____

_____

Proverbs 15:13, 30

_____

_____

Nehemiah 8:10b

_____

_____

CATECHISM EXCERPTS | *for reflection*

Now do the same for the *Catechism* excerpts. Note in your journal your insights and anything new you haven't realized before about the gift of joy.

CCC, 301

_____

_____

CCC, 736

_____

_____

CCC, 1832

_____

_____

TIMELESS | TRUTHS   *Cheryl*

Discussion Questions

1. How would you define joy? How does it differ from happiness?
2. In what ways do you experience and reflect joy?
3. Is a joyful attitude part of your everyday life? How?
4. What affect does a joyful attitude have on your relationships? Your work? Your vocation?
5. What kinds of things steal your joy?
6. What practical steps can you take to stop this from happening?
7. How does joy connect you to God?
8. How can you be joyful in the midst of difficulties or tragedy?

① Joy - deeper feeling
Happiness - fleeting

⑦ Inner peace

⑧ Faith

MY | PERSONAL | TAKEAWAY

transformative - Joy

Not Conformed, but Transformed
Phil Ch 4 V 4
Psalm 118

Proverbs Ch 17 V 22

Joy is attitude
Matthew C 16 V 24-25

Joy lies w/in God

life is participation in God

Paul - I Corin Ch 1 V 9

James Ch 1 V 2-3

Evening - reflect on day - 3 min

Phil 6 Ch V 5

Matt C 25 V 34-30

Jesus comes first!

TIMELY | TRUTHS   *Teresa*

Rejoice in the Lord always; again I will say, Rejoice.

—Philippians 4:4

The *fruits* of charity are joy, peace, and mercy.

—CCC, 1829

If you want to evangelize well, start with a big smile. Be joyful. Be kind. We're told in 1 Peter 3:15, "Always be prepared to make a defense to any one who calls you to account for the hope that is in you, yet do it with gentleness and reverence." One of my personal favorite quotes about turning those frowns upside down comes from the feisty St. Teresa of Avila, the first female doctor of the Church. "Lord, preserve us from sour-faced saints." No wonder she was known not only for her great teaching and mysticism but also for her dynamic, outgoing, and fun-loving personality.

Taking a positive or joyful approach does not mean you should walk around in la-la land, ignoring the problems you may have in your own life or in the world around you. However, it does mean that you won't be thrown off course every time trouble rears its ugly head and tries to toss you around like a toy boat in a giant swimming pool. This is the difference between joy and happiness. Joy is truly the gift that keeps on giving. Happiness is fleeting and much more dependent on feelings. Being joyful is a way of life.

SCRIPTURES | *for reflection*

Look up each verse and read it slowly and prayerfully. What do you sense God saying to you about his gift of joy for you? Write your answers in your journal.

John 16:24

_____

_____

Acts 13:48–52

_____

_____

1 Thessalonians 5:16

_____

_____

CATECHISM EXCERPTS | *for reflection*

Now do the same for the *Catechism* excerpts. Note in your journal your insights and anything new you haven't realized before about the gift of joy.

CCC, 1808

_____

_____

CCC, 2639

_____

_____

CCC, 2648

_____

_____

TIMELY | TRUTHS

Teresa

Discussion Questions

1. Do you find it easy to be joyful, or is this something you struggle with?

2. Is there someone in your life who demonstrates joy in the face of hardship? List some of the ways.

3. Is there someone in your life who is always upbeat and smiling? How does this person make you feel when you're with them?

4. Contrast this with someone you know who rarely smiles. What effect does this person have on you?

5. How can whether you are joyful or not affect your physical health?

6. How can you be joyful even when you are taking a serious stand on an issue such as abortion?

7. Is there a particular situation in your life right now that you could choose to be joyful about? How might having a joyful perspective make a difference?

8. When you are feeling grumpy, what is the *best* way for you to regain your joy?

MY | PERSONAL | TAKEAWAY

_____

_____

_____

_____

_____

_____

_____

_____

_____

_____

_____

_____

_____

_____

_____

_____

_____

_____

_____

_____

_____

_____

_____

_____

_____

chapter five

THE
GIFT
OF
SUFFERING

A Prayer to Begin...

My Lord and Savior, there has been no suffering like your suffering, a suffering you willingly accepted for my sake. Give me strength as I endure the cross that has been placed in my life. Let me walk beside you, yoked to you, and join my cross to yours. Allow my gratitude to always outweigh the burden I may feel and let my humble thank-you for your cross and mine be so much more than words. Let it emanate from the depths of my soul and be pleasing to you. Amen.

TIMELESS | TRUTHS   *Cheryl*

In this you rejoice, though now for a little while you may have to suffer various trials, so that the genuineness of your faith, more precious than gold which though perishable is tested by fire, may redound to praise and glory and honor at the revelation of Jesus Christ.

—1 Peter 1:6–7

Sufferings to be endured can mean that "in my flesh I complete what is lacking in Christ's afflictions for the sake of his Body, that is, the Church."[4]

—CCC, 1508

I love attending the Stations of the Cross during Lent. For me, that forty-five minutes each Friday evening puts life completely in perspective. The dialogue, the give-and-take between the congregants and the pastor or deacon, draws me in and envelops me in a sort of verbal prayer shawl. I am filled with emotions that range from joy at the idea of heaven to gratitude for Christ's love for me to regret for the ways in which I have sinned or not obeyed God. Every time I leave the Stations of the Cross I want to do that little jump and kick that used to be on some commercial. You know, a little jump into the air and a gentle kick of your feet together showing great jubilation for something—which seems the opposite of suffering, I know.

But somehow, after attending the Stations of the Cross, I realize how my suffering molds me, how my suffering can be joined to the cross. Most importantly, I also am reminded of the other side of the cross: the resurrection. And that is the perspective that is, as they say in yet another commercial: priceless.

Learning about "being yoked together with Christ" has been a critical piece of my suffering. Sometimes, when I feel that my suffering is too much, I envision myself in that yoke and I just completely fall into it. I allow myself to be pulled along, maybe even see my feet dragging, because I know that Christ has fit my yoke specifically to me and that being yoked to him means that he can carry me when my spirit wanes, when my suffering seems too much to bear.

During the Stations of the Cross, although knowing the answer is "nothing," Christ rhetorically asks, "What have I done or failed to do?" In those words my suffering takes on new meaning. Christ asks, "Has there been any suffering like my suffering?" and in an instant my burden becomes light. I am transformed as the words wash over me. Christ is asking each of us to be transformed by our suffering. When we consider what he has done for us, it seems like the very least that we can do for him.

SCRIPTURES | *for reflection*

Look up each verse and read it slowly and prayerfully. What do you sense God saying to you about suffering? Write your answers in your journal.

2 Corinthians 12:9

_____

_____

1 Peter 2:19–21

Joy is attitude

_____

James 5:13

_____

_____

CATECHISM EXCERPTS | *for reflection*

Now do the same for the *Catechism* excerpts. Note in your journal your insights and anything new you haven't realized before about suffering.

CCC, 164

_____

_____

CCC, 1501

_____

_____

CCC, 1521

_____

_____

TIMELESS|TRUTHS   *Cheryl*
Discussion Questions

1. What are some of the ways the Lord allows you to suffer?

2. Do you sense God's presence in your suffering? List some ways.

3. What do you think God might be trying to teach you through suffering?

4. How has your suffering framed your faith walk?

5. What is your response to your suffering? Are you able to praise God in the midst of your suffering? If not, how might you change this?

6. If you feel guilty for a negative response to suffering, list some ways you can release that guilt and turn toward God.

7. What has been your experience when you've attended the Stations of the Cross? What have you learned about your own suffering?

8. Read about Leah in chapter five of *Wrapped Up*. How might Leah help you embrace your suffering as a gift from God—and thus a gift you give yourself?

MY | PERSONAL | TAKEAWAY

_____

_____

_____

_____

_____

_____

_____

_____

_____

_____

_____

_____

_____

_____

_____

_____

_____

_____

_____

_____

_____

_____

_____

_____

_____

_____

TIMELY | TRUTHS   *Teresa*

We know that in everything God works for good with those who love him, who are called according to his purpose.

—Romans 8:28

In humbling himself, [Jesus] has given us an example to imitate, through his prayer he draws us to pray, and by his poverty he calls us to accept freely the privation and persecutions that may come our way.

—CCC, 520

My years in the trenches as a reporter in a big city allowed me to interview and mingle with some pretty major VIPs. I have covered presidential events and chatted with well-known Hollywood stars. However, my favorite stories were those that featured average folks who struggled greatly and used that pain to help others. There was the loving father whose beautiful daughter was killed by a drunk driver. He used his great loss to promote the work of Mothers Against Drunk Driving in the Detroit area. There was an elderly woman whose neighborhood was besieged by crime and drugs. She refused to be beaten by the bad guys, and eventually this strong, grandmotherly figure became a role model for many other struggling neighborhoods in the inner city. These are just two examples I've encountered who know what St. Paul means when he says in Romans 8:28 that "in everything God works for good with those who love him, who are called according to his purpose."

Maybe you've never thought of suffering in this way. But whatever you're going through right now could be of great benefit not only to you, but to someone else. After all, it's not a matter of *if* you're going to suffer but *when*. What matters is how you deal with it and what you do with it.

SCRIPTURES | *for reflection*

Look up each verse and read it slowly and prayerfully. What do you sense God saying to you? Write your answers in your journal.

John 16:33

---

2 Corinthians 1:3–7

Colossians 1:24–26

CATECHISM EXCERPTS | *for reflection*

Now do the same for the *Catechism* excerpts. Note in your journal your insights and anything new you haven't realized before about suffering.

CCC, 314

CCC, 324

CCC, 2091

TIMELY | TRUTHS   *Teresa*

Discussion Questions

1. When you've experienced suffering in your life, how has it shaped the direction of your life? Has it made you bitter or better?

2. Can you think of a time that you were called to suffer for someone else? Describe this.

3. List some ways this experience united you with the sufferings of Christ.

4. Think of an area where you are hurting currently. Could you offer this trial up for a specific person or purpose in your life? If so, for whom or what?

5. Describe someone you know who has used their suffering for the good of others. What did they do?

6. What was Christ's response to suffering? List some specifics of the example he set for us.

7. How is God's intention for us during times of suffering different from the evil one's intent?

8. How can you reconcile horrible suffering with a loving God?

MY | PERSONAL | TAKEAWAY

chapter six

THE
GIFT
OF
LETTING
GO

A Prayer to Begin...

Dear Father in heaven, as I strive to let go of whatever may hurt or haunt me, I beg your forgiveness for having clung to it instead of you. I ask that you wrap me in your loving embrace where your love will undoubtedly overshadow whatever attempts to hold me back where letting go becomes a gift and accepting the gift becomes a treasure. Amen.

TIMELESS|TRUTHS   *Cheryl*

Remember not the former things,
  nor consider the things of old.
Behold, I am doing a new thing;
  now it springs forth, do you not perceive it?

                                        —Isaiah 43:18–19

God created man a rational being, conferring on him the dignity of a person who can initiate and control his own actions. God willed that man should be "left in the hand of his own counsel," so that he might of his own accord seek his Creator and freely attain his full and blessed perfection by cleaving to him.

                                        —CCC, 1730

Abuses are real. They may be emotional, psychological, or physical. Often they feel as if they are crosses that will certainly crush us. But if they are in the past, they need to serve a better purpose than holding us back from the present, which is a gift from God, and the future, which has yet to be written.

For many this will involve the process of forgiveness, while for others it may require a conscious effort to turn one's heart, mind, and soul to Christ and then begin the journey of healing within the shadow of the cross. Either way, it means understanding that letting go and moving on is an important goal.

In letting go, we are able to step toward Christ who heals us and lay our hurts and angers and baggage at the foot of the cross. This allows us, then, a starting point—our own earthly resurrection—in which we will be able to enjoy God's gift of life and friendship in new and deeper ways. As wounds from the past resurface, as they surely will, we continue to lay them at the foot of the cross. We join the other women who stood by his side during the darkest hour, free from what had a claim on us so that we can proclaim the Good News of salvation in Jesus.

SCRIPTURES | *for reflection*

Look up each verse and read it slowly and prayerfully. What do you sense God saying to you? Write your answers in your journal.

Genesis 19:26

_____

_____

Mark 1:17

_____

_____

Romans 12:9

_____

_____

CATECHISM EXCERPTS | *for reflection*

Now do the same for the *Catechism* excerpts. Note in your journal your insights and anything new you haven't realized before about letting go.

CCC, 55

_____

_____

CCC, 2029

_____

_____

CCC, 2467

_____

_____

TIMELESS | TRUTHS   *Cheryl*
Discussion Questions

1. Are holding on to anything that God has asked you to release? If so, what?

2. How can you invite God to help you in the process of letting go? What are some practical steps you can take?

3. Are you clinging to disappointment, disordered desires, or pain instead of cleaving to God?

4. Consider the ways you can cleave to God: quiet prayer, attending Mass on a regular basis, daily rosary, joining a Bible study. Choose one or two that you can commit to, and write them down here.

5. How has letting go in the past deepened your relationship with God? In what ways did you grow?

6. Are there areas of remorse over past mistakes that still hold you back today? What are they?

7. How can you let go of these areas and experience freedom?

8. Think of something small you could give up that will assist you to let go of bigger things that hold you back. What might you choose?

MY | PERSONAL | TAKEAWAY

TIMELY | TRUTHS   *Teresa*

One thing I do, forgetting what lies behind and straining forward
to what lies ahead, I press on toward the goal for the prize of the
upward call of God in Christ Jesus.

—Philippians 3:13–14

Within modern society the communications media play a major
role in information, cultural promotion, and formation. This role
is increasing, as a result of technological progress, the extent and
diversity of the news transmitted, and the influence exercised on
public opinion.

—CCC, 2493

At a certain point in my life, I knew I had to leave secular media
and see what God might have in mind. About a year later the radio
station was getting ready to make some on-air adjustments. The
station manager was gracious enough to buy out the remainder of
my contract and allow me to exit gracefully. That's when I finally
let go and said, "Whatever, Lord." I could almost hear the Lord
saying in return, "Okay, now you're ready."

I walked away from secular media in February 2000 feeling very
peaceful about my decision. In prayer, I told God that I would go
wherever he wanted to send me and do whatever he wanted me to
do, but he needed to show me the way. Within a few short months,
I was hired by the local evangelical station and given my own daily
talk show. The on-air exposure allowed me to build contacts within
the local faith community. Speaking requests started to come in,
and two years later I was hired by a Catholic radio network.

So what is the plan, the idea, the goal to which you're clinging so
tightly? It may be the very thing blocking the truly abundant life

that could be yours. When are you going to trust the Lord enough
to let go and release it all to God, recognizing this as a true gift that
can help you move forward?

SCRIPTURES | *for reflection*

Look up each verse and read it slowly and prayerfully. What do you sense God saying to you? Write your answers in your journal.

Proverbs 3:5-6

_____

_____

Matthew 4:18-22

_____

_____

John 8:32

_____

_____

CATECHISM EXCERPTS | *for reflection*

Now do the same for the *Catechism* excerpts. Note in your journal your insights and anything new you haven't realized before about letting go.

CCC, 1694

_____

_____

CCC, 2134

_____

_____

CCC, 2494

_____

_____

TIMELY | TRUTHS
Discussion Questions

Teresa

1. Do you set specific goals regularly for yourself? If so, what are they? If not, why not?

2. How does your faith impact your attitude toward your goals and dreams?

3. Describe the balance between taking initiative in pursuing your plans and being able to let go and let God. How does this practically play out in your life?

4. What have you struggled to let go of? Why has this been so difficult?

5. What has been your experience with letting go? Describe a time when you chose to let go of something. What was the result?

6. Do you really trust that God has better plans for you than you could dream up for yourself? Or is there a part of you that holds back, afraid that you will be unhappy if you allow him to have his way in your life?

7. Can you think of a real-life example of someone who demonstrates "letting go and letting God"? What does that person's life look like?

8. Is there something in your life that you can release right now? Do it now—and then note any immediate results here.

The War Room

MY | PERSONAL | TAKEAWAY

Washing dishes & hands w/ Statue
(Our Lady of the sink)

Our Lady of the washing machine

Reading book

Aux member - Legion of Mary
prayers

Spiritual walk outside
+ FB - spiritual message

Dynamic Catholic - email

Liturgy of the hour

EWTN

Laudato

Shrines - visit

Holy Door - visit

Adoration
Stations of the Cross
Lunch & Learn
Bible Study

THE
GIFT
OF
A
SACRAMENTAL
LIFE

A Prayer to Begin...

Lord Jesus Christ, in becoming my sustenance you also become my substance, and for that I am eternally grateful. With your help my life can truly become sacramental; it will be both whole and holy. I desire all the details of my life—great and small—to be for your greater glory and for my own salvation. Washed in your precious blood, I can do all things you call me to do. Amen.

TIMELESS | TRUTHS   *Cheryl*

Let the words of my mouth and the meditation of my heart
  be acceptable in your sight,
  O LORD, my rock and my redeemer.

—Psalm 19:14

By free will one shapes one's own life. Human freedom is a force for
growth and maturity in truth and goodness; it attains its perfection
when directed toward God, our beatitude.

—*CCC*, 1731

After attending an Ignatian retreat for the purpose of seeking God's
will in my life and better discerning God's movements in my life,
I knew God was calling me to set aside time that could be devoted
entirely to him.

Recognizing that "time aside for God" could be a bit ephemeral
without some sort of conscious act associated with it, I created a
little prayer corner in the upstairs hallway of my home. I purchased
a small kneeler from a church supply store and repurposed a narrow
bookshelf that had been in my front room. I placed the kneeler
in front of the bookshelf which was now filled with icons I had
collected over the years. I purchased some votive candles and
used a small, beautifully hand-painted bowl to hold the different
medallions I had also collected. A pretty rose-covered box became
home to the many prayer pamphlets and Mass cards I had amassed.
The bottom cupboard portion of the unit housed my novena books,
a Bible, and some other favorite reading materials.

The establishment of the prayer corner was my way of living my
life in a very sacramental way. My intent is to live the time I give

over to God purposefully while also living it joyfully. Setting this time aside for God has had a powerful impact on me.

A friend recently brought to our Bible Study a pillow shaped somewhat like a head and shoulders. It was about twelve inches wide and maybe fifteen inches high. It had a picture of Our Lady of Perpetual Help adorning the front. On the back were the words for the corresponding prayer. The pillow was made as part of a ministry that tended to elderly patients in nursing homes and other situations. The idea? Give the patients something to have and to hold—to hug.

Honoring the way we are created as beings that enjoy, need, want, and even desire a tangible way to practice our faith means we live it sacramentally. Whether we are purposely setting aside time and a sacred space to heighten our awareness of the indwelling God, or gazing upon an icon, or hugging a pillow with a depiction of Mary, we experience the richness of who we are because of these tangible sacramentals. They don't become idols to us; rather, they satisfy the God-given senses we all have. They help manifest a fuller understanding of our faith and our creator as we take him in as best we can. Living sacramentally allows us to deal with seeing through a glass darkly until we see face-to-face (see 1 Corinthians 13:12).

SCRIPTURES | *for reflection*

Look up each verse and read it slowly and prayerfully. What do you sense God saying to you? Write your answers in your journal.

Deuteronomy 26:1–2

_____

_____

Psalm 96:9

_____

_____

Matthew 6:6

_____

_____

CATECHISM EXCERPTS | *for reflection*

Now do the same for the *Catechism* excerpts. Note in your journal your insights about what it means to live sacramentally.

CCC, 1146

_____

_____

CCC, 1667

_____

_____

CCC, 1674

_____

_____

TIMELESS│TRUTHS   *Cheryl*

Discussion Questions

1. What are the benefits of setting aside a special time for God?
2. Do you have a prayer corner in your home? If so, what does it look like? What things have you placed there?
3. What results have you noticed in your life because of having a prayer corner?
4. If you don't have a prayer corner, how could you create one? Where in your home would you set this up, and what kinds of items would you include in it?
5. How would you define a "sacramental" life?
6. How do you personally live sacramentally?
7. What are the benefits of living a sacramental life?
8. Name an area where you sense God is calling you to live in a more deeply sacramental way. How will you do this?

The Teressa

CWA—
Wed 1:30
16ᵃ + lunch

Living in Christ:

MY | PERSONAL | TAKEAWAY

Confession: every day faults

② Being faithful to prayer life

Have I done this to live a more
sacrificial life?

① short or frustration w/ husband
② by my standards

Have I truly listened to him?
Have I listened to elderly

Have I been judgmental?
Did I give time just to God
today?

Gossiping

Thank you to service people

Prayer for enemies

Spiritual Director ~ confession

good habit = virtues

TIMELY | TRUTHS   *Teresa*

For everything created by God is good, and nothing is to be rejected if it is received with thanksgiving; for then it is consecrated by the word of God and prayer.

—1 Timothy 4:4–5

"The beauty of the images moves me to contemplation, as a meadow delights the eyes and subtly infuses the soul with the glory of God." Similarly, the contemplation of sacred icons, united with meditation on the Word of God and the singing of liturgical hymns, enters into the harmony of the signs of celebration so that the mystery celebrated is imprinted in the heart's memory and is then expressed in the new life of the faithful.[5]

—CCC, 1162

When I was a little girl, I spent hours, especially during the summer months, sitting up in the huge poplar tree in our backyard. I absolutely loved to pass the time by watching the sun sparkle through the leaves. I also loved the smell of tree branches and the scent of the freshly mowed lawn below. If you had asked me then, I probably couldn't have explained it in a spiritual sense, but I did feel a great connection to God up there. I had a sense of just how beautiful the world was. I was in awe of what I saw around me and didn't want to miss a thing. I guess you could say in some ways I was already living a sacramental life.

We are not just spiritual beings floating around on the earth on our way to heaven. We are body and soul made in God's image and likeness. Jesus was fully God and fully man. Embracing the gift of a sacramental life enables us to understand the beauty of all that

God created, namely the creation he loves the most: you and me. Embracing the gift of a sacramental life means to appreciate life in all its forms.

Over the years I have known some Christians who shy away from the term *sacrament* or *sacramental*. Some might have felt embracing this gift would mean becoming too worldly or putting too much emphasis on material things. Some put the idea of sacrament aside completely because it's a "Catholic" thing. But in its truest sense, a sacramental life means understanding the beauty of God's design in everything. If it is applied correctly, it can lead us to a closer relationship to God because it allows us to see him in all things, much as St. Francis explains in his Canticle of the Creatures: "All praise be yours, my Lord, through all that you have made."

God came to us through the Incarnation as a man. Our bodies are not bad, neither are the treasures and pleasures of physical life such as food, clothing, art, and music. All in moderation can be used for good means, and this is what the sacramental life is meant to be. For Catholic Christians in particular, the seven sacraments of the Catholic Church, which are applied through physical means or practices, help us embrace the spiritual.

God's handiwork is always present and is often crying out to us from multiple sources and levels. It is present in our individual gifts, in the words of his most dedicated followers, in Scripture, and in the sacraments of the Catholic Church, most importantly the source and summit of the Catholic faith: Holy Communion. We just have to have eyes to see, ears to hear, and hearts open to receive.

SCRIPTURES | *for reflection*

Look up each verse and read it slowly and prayerfully. What do you sense God saying to you? Write your answers in your journal.

Matthew 3:13–17

_____

_____

John 4:1–42

_____

_____

John 9:1–6

_____

_____

CATECHISM EXCERPTS | *for reflection*

Now do the same for the *Catechism* excerpts. Note in your journal your insights about living sacramentally.

CCC, 1159

_____

_____

CCC, 1161

_____

_____

CCC, 1670

_____

_____

TIMELY│TRUTHS   *Teresa*
Discussion Questions

1. What is your view of the sacraments of the Catholic Church and how can they help sanctify us?

2. Have you ever had a problem with applying the idea of a sacramental life to your own daily walk with Jesus? Describe this.

3. Describe some scenes in Jesus's life where he used the physical to explain the spiritual. How did Jesus help others see the importance of living a sacramental life?

4. What things in the natural world help you to develop a sacramental approach to living?

5. What can we learn about God from being sacramental and from the seven sacraments of the Catholic Church?

6. How can you keep material things in perspective when there is so much excess in our culture?

7. Look around you today. What surrounds you that speaks to you of God's presence in the world?

8. As you receive Holy Communion next time, ask God to open your heart in a new way to receive Christ in a more sacramental way. Record in your journal how this made a difference.

MY | PERSONAL | TAKEAWAY

chapter eight

THE
GIFT
OF
YOUR
SISTERS
IN
FAITH

A Prayer to Begin...

Father, in your Son I have a brother. And through my brother, I have been given many sisters in faith. What a gift! How many lives are meant to converge for your kingdom and accomplish your work! Thank you for counting me among the sisters in faith and for helping me to see the beautiful potential that exists in every single woman whose path crosses with mine. Let me not see friend or foe, my agenda or hers; let me not judge nor allow others to judge me, but simply let me see my sisters with your eyes—the eyes of love. Amen.

TIMELESS | TRUTHS   *Cheryl*

Beloved, let us love one another; for love is of God, and he who loves is born of God and knows God.

—1 John 4:7

The first man was not only created good, but was also established in friendship with his Creator and in harmony with himself and with the creation around him, in a state that would be surpassed only by the glory of the new creation in Christ.

—CCC, 374

One of my favorite women from Scripture is Noah's wife. She quickly became my role model when my three sons were smaller and it seemed like I was barely keeping up with the demands of caring for them, my home, my husband, and my job. Contemplating life on the ark became, for me, something that made me smile—and sometimes cringe.

Imagine what life on the ark was like: dark, dirty, dingy, stinky, exhausting, to be sure. In the day-to-day grind of saving mankind, caring for the family and the animals must have been truly grueling. And without the missus, we can be sure that Noah's endeavor would not have been successful. (I'm just saying...)

This has taught me a lot about my sisters-in-faith. I have learned that the best way to look at them is to look at them through the understanding of Noah's wife. This means I see them as women who are typically busy manning an ark. They are embroiled in the day-to-day life of saving mankind one person at a time—typically a child or a neighbor or a colleague. They are probably fairly anonymous, just as Noah's wife remained anonymous even while her work was monumental. (Again, I'm just saying...)

I believe that if we each look at one another as a mini-Noah's wife, we can better learn to love and embrace one another. We can better learn to build up one another. When we see the real women behind the façades that are our daily lives, we see in each other a mirror of ourselves: simply women working for God and his kingdom amid a raging storm.

Today, we live in an age where we are connected to countless others. We have to be guided by God and ask that we be his instruments and not take lightly the new world that is open to us. We should lovingly and cautiously create a sisterhood unlike any other—a sisterhood where we will meet in the valleys between our mountains and recognize how we each are uniquely created and gifted as daughters of the King and thus love and care for one another. It is a huge responsibility, to be sure, but we are up to the challenge!

Sisters in Faith

SCRIPTURES | *for reflection*

Look up each verse and read it slowly and prayerfully. What do you sense God saying to you? Write your answers in your journal.

Successful retrats

Psalm 37:11

Prayer without ceasing

Lamentations 21:1

1 Thessalonians 5:17

CATECHISM EXCERPTS | *for reflection*

Now do the same for the *Catechism* excerpts. Note in your journal your insights and anything new you haven't realized before about the gift of sisters in faith.

CCC, 358

CCC, 369-373 *Willed you into being*

CCC, 2010 *Do Nothing to merit God's grace*

TIMELESS | TRUTHS

Cheryl

Discussion Questions

1. How do you connect with the people God has put in your life?

2. Are you too connected to the digital world and not connected enough to your real world?

3. How is humility expressed in your relationships with your sisters in faith?

4. Think of a time when you struggled with a relationship with one of your sisters. How did you resolve this?

5. Now think of a time when a fellow sister encouraged you during a difficult time. What did she say or do that helped you?

6. Is developing relationships with your Christian sisters a priority for you? If not, why not?

7. How can you take steps to deepen your friendships in Christ?

8. Can you think of a particular sister in faith who might need some attention? Think of a practical way you can show love to her.

What legacy will you leave?

MY | PERSONAL | TAKEAWAY

_____
_____
_____
_____
_____
_____
_____
_____
_____
_____
_____
_____
_____
_____
_____
_____
_____
_____
_____
_____
_____
_____
_____
_____
_____
_____
_____
_____

TIMELY|TRUTHS   *Teresa*

Walk in a manner worthy of the calling to which you have been called, with all lowliness and meekness, with patience, forbearing one another in love, eager to maintain the unity of the Spirit in the bond of peace.

—Ephesians 4:1–3

"This law of human solidarity and charity," without excluding the rich variety of persons, cultures, and peoples, assures us that all men are truly brethren.[6]

—CCC, 361

One of the best examples of how the gift of sisterhood manifests itself in my life is through my work as a Catholic pilgrimage host. All types of people from all parts of the world join us in Rome or the Holy Land. Some are outgoing. Some are more reserved. But all are believers in Christ, adopted sons and daughters, and therefore truly brothers and sisters. There is an instantaneous connection because of the presence of God. It really is an example of the Holy Spirit doing some of his best work.

As a result of these trips, I now have family in many cities. Not only do these fine folks keep in touch with me, they often host me in their homes when I come to town for speaking events. In the last year, for example, I have caught up with these "relatives" of mine on at least three or four separate occasions.

I am so grateful for this gift, especially now as our increasingly secularized society is becoming more and more hostile to people of faith. What a gift it is to know we have real sisters who share our love of the Lord and who can walk with us through the ups and downs of life.

SCRIPTURES | *for reflection*

Look up each verse and read it slowly and prayerfully. What do you sense God saying to you? Write your answers in your journal.

Luke 10:38–42

_____

_____

John 19:25–27

_____

_____

Philippians 2:7

_____

_____

CATECHISM EXCERPTS | *for reflection*

Now do the same for the *Catechism* excerpts. Note in your journal your insights and anything new you haven't realized before about the gift of sisters in faith.

CCC, 27

_____

_____

CCC, 1935

_____

_____

CCC, 2012

_____

_____

TIMELY | TRUTHS   *Teresa*

Discussion Questions

1. Who are the "sisters" in your life?
2. How did you come to identify these women as sisters?
3. Where did you meet these sisters (church, Bible study, work, school)?
4. How do you see the gift of sisters in faith revealed in Scripture, particularly in the Gospels?
5. How did Jesus encourage friendship among those to whom he ministered?
6. How did Jesus help the sisterhood between Martha and Mary?
7. How do you think the experiences of the women who were with Jesus at the cross and then the grave grew in their sisterhood?
8. How do the situations in your life, both positive ones and those that are challenging, help to deepen your relationships with your sisters in faith?

MY | PERSONAL | TAKEAWAY

chapter nine

THE
GIFT
OF
SETTING
PRIORITIES

A Prayer to Begin...

Jesus, you made me a priority in your life; please help me make you a priority in mine. Stay with me as I sift through things that I believe matter but really don't. Guide me as I struggle to commit to things that will bring me closer to you but are far too easy to abandon. You never abandoned me, my Lord and Savior—never allow me to abandon you! Amen.

TIMELESS | TRUTHS   *Cheryl*

You shall love the Lord your God with all your heart, and with all your soul, and with all your mind, and with all your strength.

—Mark 12:30

By faith, man completely submits his intellect and his will to God. With his whole being man gives his assent to God the revealer. Sacred Scripture calls this human response to God, the author of revelation, "the obedience of faith."[7]

—CCC, 143

Most of us know that we ought to find time for God, our prayer life, our family, our friends, and the countless demands placed upon our lives, but few of us take the time to make it our goal to set the right priorities. We juggle, we fret, we get into a groove, and we coast, all the while wanting, needing, and recognizing how important our relationship with God is and knowing it should be our first priority.

But what does it really mean to spend time with God? I know that when I clean or cook or iron (yuk!), I am always talking to God. I don't think I've ever walked the local track without my arms waving and my lips moving (much to the dismay of the other walkers) because I am always in conversation with God. He is a very real part of all I do. And, on occasion, he gets a word in edgewise.

While God is very much a part of our everyday lives, it behooves us to carve out time that is devoted solely to him. It is only in making him our top priority that we recognize the futility of trying to accomplish all that is on our plate. God is a master at time management, and his Son's peace, unlike any worldly peace, comes from time devoted to him each and every day.

SCRIPTURES | *for reflection*

Look up each verse and read it slowly and prayerfully. What do you sense God saying to you? Write your answers in your journal.

Exodus 20:1–3

_____

_____

2 Kings 23:25

_____

_____

1 John 5:5

_____

_____

CATECHISM EXCERPTS | *for reflection*

Now do the same for the *Catechism* excerpts. Note in your journal your insights and anything new you haven't realized before about priorities.

CCC, 260

_____

_____

CCC, 2083

_____

_____

CCC, 2087

_____

_____

TIMELESS | TRUTHS   *Cheryl*

Discussion Questions

1. As you go through your daily routines, do you carry on a conversation with God? If you don't, how can you become more mindful of him?

2. How does the world's definition of productivity differ from the way God defines it?

3. Why is it important to set aside undivided chunks of time to spend time in prayer?

4. What is on your plate these days? Is it filled with more than any one woman could accomplish?

5. If you answered yes to question four, what caused this situation to happen?

6. What might the Holy Spirit be whispering to you as you reflect on your answer to question four? Do you need to make some changes?

7. What are some specific ways you can implement your desire to make God your first priority?

8. When you have made time alone with God a priority, what results have you seen in your life?

MY | PERSONAL | TAKEAWAY

_____

_____

_____

_____

_____

_____

_____

_____

_____

_____

_____

_____

_____

_____

_____

_____

_____

_____

_____

_____

_____

_____

_____

TIMELY | TRUTHS

Teresa

But the Lord answered her, "Martha, Martha, you are anxious and troubled about many things; one thing is needful. Mary has chosen the good portion, which shall not be taken away from her."

—Luke 10:41–42

Just as God "rested on the seventh day from all his work which he had done," human life has a rhythm of work and rest.[8]

—CCC, 2184

The Italians have a saying: "*Il dolce far niente.*" Translated this means the art or sweetness of doing nothing. And it Italy it really is an art, particularly around the time of the Italians' main meal of the day, called "pranzo." They know how to relax, enjoy their delicious food and wine, and spend time doing nothing—yes, *nothing.* Having had the blessing of visiting Italy often, I have also noticed that this art of doing nothing also includes sitting in the local piazza or strolling along the winding streets in the colorful cities and hill towns. This art of doing nothing is really doing something for the mind, body, and soul; it appears to be a true time of reflection and relaxation.

This might seem like sacrilege to most Americans who run around from task to task and sound a lot like the White Rabbit from Alice in Wonderland: "I'm late. I'm late for a very important date. No time to say hello because I'm late. I'm late. I'm late." We too often equate business with productivity and success, and doing nothing with...well, the losers and the procrastinators. In Italy, however, *il dolce far niente* is at the top of most people's priority list. Wouldn't it be nice if we had a new American saying like, "Don't just do something, sit there"?

So what does doing nothing have to do with setting priorities? Well, frankly, everything. A big problem for many of us today is that we have plenty of things on our to-do lists, but most of those lists include everyday chores, tasks, and responsibilities that have little if anything to do with the conditions of our souls. This is not to say that taking care of our homes and families and keeping our commitments isn't important. But that said, women tend to take care of everyone else before taking care of themselves. We need to prioritize so we can set time aside to be alone with God and ourselves—and time for learning the art of doing nothing.

SCRIPTURES | *for reflection*

Look up each verse and read it slowly and prayerfully. What do you sense God saying to you? Write your answers in your journal.

Proverbs 3:6

_____

_____

Matthew 6:33

_____

_____

Colossians 3:1–4

_____

_____

CATECHISM EXCERPTS | *for reflection*

Now do the same for the *Catechism* excerpts. Note in your journal your insights and anything new you haven't realized before about priorities.

CCC, 144

_____

_____

CCC, 150

_____

_____

CCC, 2096

_____

_____

TIMELY | TRUTHS   *Teresa*
Discussion Questions

1. What items are on your priority list?

2. How many of those items have to do with you and God?

3. How might you change that list to better reflect the spiritual needs in your life?

4. What do you think of the concept of "*il dolce far niente*"? Is there a part of you that feels resistance to this art of doing nothing? If so, why?

5. How did Jesus prioritize his life in terms of giving himself time alone?

6. Read the story of Mary and Martha in Luke 10:38–42. What did Jesus teach about priorities?

7. List some ways that taking care of the most important relationship in your life—your relationship with Jesus—might have positive benefits in your health and well-being.

8. Create an "*il dolce far niente*" day for yourself. Where will you go? How will your spend that time?

MY | PERSONAL | TAKEAWAY

---

c h a p t e r   t e n

THE
GIFT
OF
YOU!

A Prayer to Begin...

Father, how easy it is for me to forget that you gave your Son for my sake! I often forget the special place I have in your heart and how much you value me. For that I seek your forgiveness, and I ask that you allow me to start today, new and fresh, in my understanding and belief that I am loved by you. Help me to accept my own preciousness as a priceless gift! Amen.

TIMELESS | TRUTHS *Cheryl*

But you are a chosen race, a royal priesthood, a holy nation, God's own people, that you may declare the wonderful deeds of him who called you out of darkness into his marvelous light.

—1 Peter 2:9

God loves his people more than a bridegroom his beloved; his love will be victorious over even the worst infidelities and will extend to his most precious gift: "God so loved the world that he gave his only Son."[9]

—CCC, 219

In *Mulieris Dignitatem*, John Paul II speaks of the "feminine genius" that we all share as daughters of the King. It is high time for us to be wrapped up in Christ's arms and embrace who we are! Being a daughter of the King is a noble calling; it involves understanding how to serve God in whatever capacity we find ourselves.

Daughters of the King fill myriad roles with faith and hope and trust. A daughter of the King has an inherent worth that she does well to embrace and enjoy. She does not relinquish her status as a princess, but receives it graciously as a gift and lives accordingly.

A daughter of the King brings great things to the world in which she lives! She witnesses to the abundant love and salvation found in Jesus. She desires a life of hope and joy. She pursues wisdom so that she may give it and receive it. As a daughter of the King, her influence is without bounds wherever she finds herself, and she recognizes the need to wield that influence for God and his kingdom.

There is no greater knowledge, no higher call, than for each of us to recognize our standing as a daughter of the King!

SCRIPTURES | *for reflection*

Look up each verse and read it slowly and prayerfully. What do you sense God saying to you? Write your answers in your journal.

Judith 8:7–8

_____

_____

Matthew 9:18–22

_____

_____

John 20:14–16

_____

_____

CATECHISM EXCERPTS | *for reflection*

Now do the same for the *Catechism* excerpts. Note in your journal your insights and anything new you haven't realized before about how priceless you are in God's eyes.

CCC, 301

_____

_____

CCC, 358

_____

_____

CCC, 733

_____

_____

TIMELESS│TRUTHS   *Cheryl*

Discussion Questions

1. Name five characteristics you like about yourself (be bold and don't hide behind false humility) that you recognize as gifts from God.

2. How might God being trying to mold those characteristics in a way that they become even more valuable to you and to him?

3. What characteristics would you like to change about yourself? Why?

4. Examine your reasons—are they selfish (for you) or selfless (for God)?

5. What resistance do you encounter in yourself regarding areas you know you need to change? Why?

6. How does seeing yourself as a daughter of the King influence your daily habits?

7. How does seeing yourself as a daughter of the King make a difference in your relationships?

8. Name some specific ways you can better respond to God's promptings.

MY | PERSONAL | TAKEAWAY

TIMELY | TRUTHS *Teresa*

You shall love the Lord your God with all your heart, and with all your soul, and with all your mind, and with all your strength

—Mark 12:30

Christ...makes man fully manifest to man himself and brings to light his exalted vocation.[10]

—CCC, 1710

A few years ago I came across something called "God's Love Letter" or "The Father's Love Letter" (www.fathersloveletter.com). Someone very clever decided to compile many of the Scripture verses that express God's love for man and put them in the form of a love letter. Given that we live in a day and age when girls start dieting as young as eight and when some women believe that plastic surgery is the only way to get a man and keep a job, we might be in dire need for a refresher course on just how much we are loved by our creator. In addition, many children today are growing up without fathers, and positive images of fathers have all but disappeared from our mass media.

Two truths I always share when speaking to women and girls at my various conferences and events are:

- God doesn't make junk.
- Remember that you are a daughter of the King of kings.

We can't love anyone else if we don't first love ourselves, and we can forget about accepting God's love if we don't see ourselves as worthy of being loved. Ponder, pray, and reflect on just some of the many verses concerning the Lord's love and be comforted in knowing you serve a God whose love is unconditional, never-ending, and always there for you.

SCRIPTURES | *for reflection*

Look up each verse and read it slowly and prayerfully. What do you sense God saying to you? Write your answers in your journal.

Psalm 139

_____

_____

Jeremiah 1:4–5

_____

_____

1 John 3:1

_____

_____

CATECHISM EXCERPTS | *for reflection*

Now do the same for the *Catechism* excerpts. Note in your journal your insights and anything new you haven't realized before about how priceless you are in God's eyes.

CCC, 64

_____

_____

CCC, 356

_____

_____

CCC, 489

_____

_____

TIMELY | TRUTHS
Discussion Questions

Teresa

1. Do you really see yourself as a treasured daughter of the King? If not, why not?
2. What are some steps you can take to become more aware of the way God sees you?
3. How much of your self-doubt is due to past hurts? What are they?
4. What pressures from outside sources such as media or peer pressure cause you to doubt yourself and God's love for you?
5. Name at least three ways in which you see yourself as God's gift.
6. What are some ways you can help those in your family see how much God values them?
7. Whom do you know who needs to hear that she is a daughter of the King, highly valued and loved?
8. What can you do for this person to show her God's love? Think of one small way.

MY | PERSONAL | TAKEAWAY

_____

_____

_____

_____

_____

_____

_____

_____

_____

_____

_____

_____

_____

_____

_____

_____

_____

_____

_____

_____

_____

_____

_____

_____

_____

Notes

1. See Galatians 5:25; Philippians 2:1, 5; quoting Ephesians 4:32.
2. See Luke 15; 19:9.
3. "Forgiveness Boosts Health," *Arthritis Today Magazine*, www.arthritis.org/forgiveness-boosts-health.php.
4. Quoting 2 Corinthians 12:9; Colossians 1:24.
5. Quoting St. John Damascene, *De sacris imaginibus orationes* 1, 27: J.P. Migne, ed., *Patrologia Graeca* (Paris, 1857–1866), 94, 1268A, B.
6. Quoting Pius XII, *Summi Pontificatus*, 3.
7. See *Dei Verbum*, 5; see also Romans 1:5; 16:26.
8. Quoting Genesis 2:2.
9. Quoting John 3:16; see Hosea 11:1; Isaiah 49:14–15; 62:4–5; Ezekiel 16; Hosea 11.
10. Quoting *Gaudium et Spes*, 22.1.